POCKET FACTS
Mountains

Philip Steele

HEINEMANN

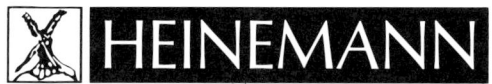

The magic of the mountains

Standing at the foot of a high mountain, people cannot help feeling a sense of awe. Buildings are dwarfed by the snowy peaks, which tower into the clouds. Mountains are often beautiful, dangerous and wild. It is easy to see why many ancient peoples believed that mountain peaks were the home of the gods. We measure mountains on land according to their height above sea-level. Surveyors measure the angle of the summit and work out its height. The most accurate measurements are taken by satellites in space. Some mountains rise from the ocean floor. Their peaks may form islands. Groups of mountains are called ranges or chains.

How mountains are formed

Mountains are formed by powerful movements inside the Earth. Our planet is a great ball of metal and rock, in both liquid and solid state. The surface, or crust, is a thin layer of solid rock. This is cracked and its sections, or plates, drift and collide. Some rocks are pushed upwards to form mountains. Others are pushed downwards to form liquid magma.

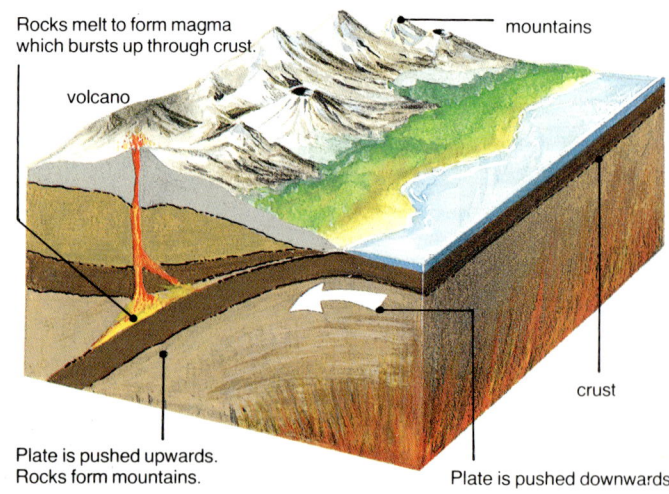

Slipping and sliding

The movements of the Earth are very slow. The folding, pushing and shoving takes millions of years. New layers of rocks may be formed beneath oceans from the remains of animals and plants. These in turn may be folded and pushed. Some sections may slip and sink, along lines called faults. Other sections called block mountains may be raised or tipped upwards.

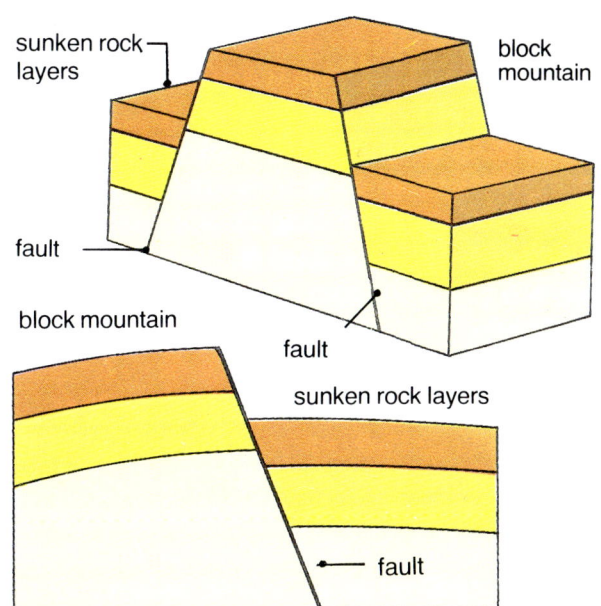

Looking at rocks

The study of rocks and their formation is called geology. Geologists look at cliffs and rock faces in order to find out how old they are. They see how the layers of rock have been twisted and folded (left). They look for the remains or shapes of ancient creatures embedded in the rocks. These fossils may tell them if the mountain was once submerged beneath the waves. The newest ranges of mountains are the highest.

Mountains in the making

Geologists can trace the history of the rocks over 3000 million years. It is a never-ending story, for today the Earth is still being re-shaped. In 1980 Mount St Helens (below), in the American state of Washington, was blown apart by a massive explosion which could be heard 500 kilometres away. A great hollow was left where there was once a peak.

Natural fireworks

The Hawaiian Islands, in the Pacific Ocean, are formed from the peaks of volcanoes which rise from the ocean floor. Some still explode, or erupt (left).
Red hot magma, called lava, bursts through the Earth's crust and streams down the mountain side. Rocks and cinders are flung into the air. Hot gases rise and meet cooler air. Clouds form, and rain may fall, causing mud slides. There are 850 active volcanoes in the world today.

Types of volcano

When lava cools, it turns into solid rock. Over the ages it forms cone-shaped mountains. Each time the volcano erupts, the top may be blasted off, or collapse inwards to form a crater.

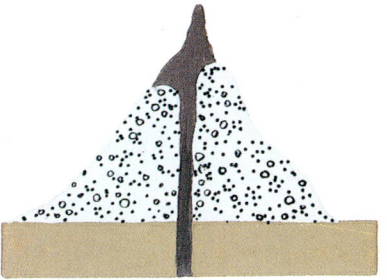

▲ This cone-shaped volcano has a crater filled with ash and lava.

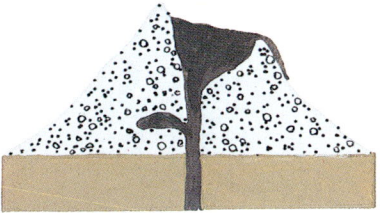

▲ This kind of volcano is plugged with lava. It erupts with force.

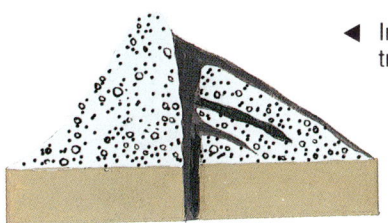

◀ In some volcanoes the lava trickles gently down the side.

▼ Lava may flood out over a wide area. It hardens to form slabs of rock.

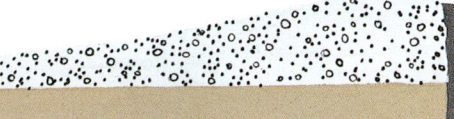

After the blast

When a volcano erupts it may destroy whole towns. However, the black soil left behind (right) is often very good for growing crops. For this reason farmers may return to the slopes of a volcano. Many volcanoes no longer erupt. They are said to be extinct. Many famous mountains are extinct volcanoes.

Ground out by ice

If many mountains are born in the fire of volcanic eruptions, many are also shaped by ice. Whole rivers of ice (right) slide down the tallest mountains. These rivers are known as glaciers. Glaciers move very slowly. They may edge forward by just a few centimetres each day. As they move, they wear down the rocks.

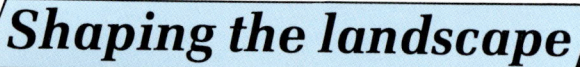

Shaping the landscape

The Yosemite valley (left) is in California, in the United States. It was carved out by glaciers about 10 000 years ago. The walls of the valley are over 900 metres high. At various periods in the Earth's history, it has been much colder than it is today. During these Ice Ages, ice spread outwards from the poles. In the Yosemite valley, the Merced River became a mighty glacier. It shaped the mountains we see there today. Many mountains still bear signs of the Ice Ages.

Lakes and inlets

When the Ice Ages ended, many glaciers melted. The valleys they had carved out filled with water. Today they form deep mountain lakes. In some places the valleys ran towards the sea, which flooded in to form deep inlets. We call these inlets firths or fiords. There are many fiords in Norway (left), Canada and New Zealand.

Water and wind

Ice is not the only other force which shapes mountains. The stream on the right is in Pakistan. It carries melting snow down from the mountain peaks. Over the ages, its fast-flowing waters have cut deeply into the rock to form a steep valley. Rainfall, rivers and water-falls all wear down, or erode, rock.

Water can eat away at rock and make it collapse. It can bore through cliffs to create natural arches and caves. The wind is another powerful force. It can blast rocks with sand and dust, and erode them into fantastic shapes. The heat of the Sun also plays its part, baking the rock face until it cracks and crumbles. Strong rocks remain while weaker ones are gradually worn away. Over the ages the weather can reduce huge peaks the size of Mount Everest to mere hills.

The snows of Kilimanjaro

When Europeans first visited Africa, they brought back tales of mountains on the Equator which were covered in snow. Few people believed them. Yet it was true. Mount Kilimanjaro (right) towers above the burning plains of Kenya and Tanzania. It is 5895 metres high. As you climb Kilimanjaro, the air becomes colder and thinner. Above 4600 metres, the rocks are covered with snow and ice.

Mountain climates

Because climate and temperature varies with height, mountain sides may include very different kinds of plant life. The picture below shows an African mountain side. On the hot lower slopes, crops such as coffee and bananas may be grown. Above this is the wet, tropical rain forest. Higher still, it is cooler and drier. Coniferous trees, such as firs and pines, grow in these tougher conditions. Soon this tree-line is left behind. Small plants give way to mosses and lichens, and then bare rock covered in snow all the year round. In other parts of the world, this pattern may vary. The lower slopes may be grazed by dairy cattle. Instead of rain forest, there may be oak or birch woods below the coniferous forests. The snow may start much lower down.

snow line
coniferous forest
rain forest
crops

Rain barriers

Mountain ranges can affect the climate of whole continents. They act as barriers against the winds blowing in from the ocean. Such winds carry a lot of water, and this means that one side of the mountain collects a heavy rain or snowfall. However the land on the other side is sheltered from the rain and winds. The lack of rain may make it into a desert.
An example of this is the western coast of North America. The coast and Cascade Ranges, and the Sierra Nevada, form a barrier to westerly winds from the Pacific Ocean. To the east of them lie dry lands and deserts.

Upland plants

The plant on the left is a giant groundsel. It is only found on the slopes of Mount Kenya, in Africa. Many plants have learned to live in harsh mountain conditions. The edelweiss is found in the Alps of Europe. It is a small plant living in rock crevices above the tree-line. Such plants are called alpines. They have a very short growing season. The edelweiss has hairy leaves to trap moisture. Other mountain plants include purple saxifrage, the gentian and the spring crocus.

Sure-footed!

High mountain peaks would hardly seem to be an ideal home for wildlife. However, many sheep and goats such as the ibex (left) have learned to survive in the mountains. They are nimble creatures and can leap from rock to rock in search of plants to nibble. Their thick coats keep them warm.

A cold-weather coat

The Tibetan Plateau is a high region sometimes known as the 'roof of the world'. It is in south-western China and is surrounded by massive ranges of mountains, including the Himalayas. Winter temperatures can drop below -40°C.
Yaks (right) are mountain oxen. They have adapted to the harsh conditions of life in the Himalayas. They are tough and sure-footed, and have shaggy coats to keep them warm. The bulls stand two metres high at the shoulder. Some yaks are wild. Others are kept in herds and used to carry loads.

Mountain cats

The rare snow leopard (below) lives in the Himalayas, the Altai and the Hindu Kush. It lives in coniferous forests at heights of up to 5500 metres. It preys on mountain goats and sheep. In the past the leopard was hunted for its fur. It is now illegal to kill one.

Bear necessities

Bears are also animals that have adapted to a life in the mountains. The grizzly bears of North America are found in Alaska (right), and in the Rocky Mountains of Canada and the United States. Some have been known to weigh over 450 kilograms. They eat plants, berries, animals and fish from mountain streams. They doze away the winter months in a snug den. A bear is protected from the bitter cold by a thick fur coat and a layer of fat.

King of the peaks

Few birds live in the mountains. The weather is harsh and the food is scarce. The golden eagle is an exception. It is found in Europe, Asia, North Africa and North America.

The golden eagle is a fine looking bird up to 90 centimetres long with a wingspan of 1.8 metres. It nests on high ledges or in tall trees. It soars to great heights, scanning the land far below for prey. It eats rabbits, ptarmigan, and animal remains.

Mountain glider

The Andean condor (below) lives in the mountains of South America. It has a wingspan of up to three metres. The rising currents of warm air over the mountains help the condor to sail high above the peaks. In this way it can search a very large area for food. Condors feed upon carrion, the remains of dead animals. If one dives to feed at a carcase, others soon follow.

Walking up walls

The wallcreeper lives in the mountains of south-eastern Europe and in Asia eastwards to the Himalayas. It is about 16 centimetres long and has claws which can grip bare rock. It can swarm up sheer cliffs in search of the insects it preys upon, or flutter out to catch them in flight. A wallcreeper has been sighted as high as 6400 metres.

The high flier

The Alpine chough (below) looks like a small crow, and is a member of the same family. It has a bright yellow beak and is well-known for its acrobatic performances when flying. It feeds on insects and other small creatures, and is often to be seen in flocks of up to 20 birds. The Alpine chough is to be found in the mountain ranges of Europe and Asia, from Spain to China. It is also found in the Atlas Mountains of North Africa. It has been seen at a height of 8200 metres in the Himalayas, where it is well known to members of expeditions climbing Mount Everest.
Alpine choughs breed in caves and crevices and on remote cliff ledges.

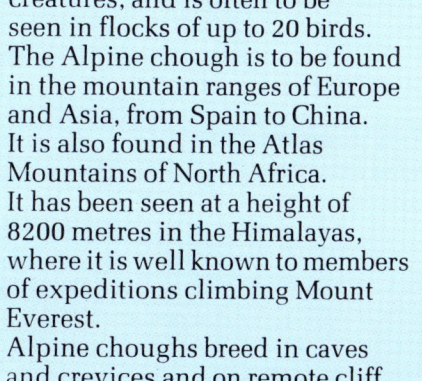

Peaks of North America

The Rocky Mountains (below) stretch from north-western Canada through the United States, joining with the Sierra Madre ranges of Mexico. The Coast Range runs along the west coast of the United States, and the Appalachians run through the eastern states.

Across a continent

The Andes Mountains stretch down the western coast of South America, from Colombia to Ecuador, Peru and Chile. The total length of the range is 6400 kilometres. In places it forms double and triple chains. Amongst the peaks are the ruins of ancient cities built by the Inca people over 500 years ago. Machu Picchu (left) can still be seen, high in the Peruvian Andes. The mountains are rich in minerals.

Old world giants

The Alps (right) form the main ranges of Western Europe. They stretch from Italy to Austria. The Pyrenees divide Spain and France. Eastern Europe is bounded by the Urals and the Caucasus, in the USSR. The main ranges of Africa include the Atlas in the north, the Ruwenzori in the east, and the southern Drakensberg mountains.

East and south

The south-western border of China is ringed by a wall of mountains. The Pamir, Karakoram and Himalaya ranges include some of the world's highest peaks. The highest mountain in Japan is the extinct volcano Fujiyama (below). Far to the south, the Great Dividing Range is Australia's longest chain. The Southern Alps form the main range of New Zealand.

Following the melting snow

Every summer the Bakhtiari people of Iran (below) take their herds up into the Zagros Mountains to graze the high pastures. When the winter snows fall, they return to the plains. All over the world, the same pattern is followed. Herds are led down into the valleys each autumn, and back to the heights each spring.

Peoples of the Andes

The Quechua people have lived in the high Andes since the days of the Incas. They grow potatoes and maize and keep sheep, llamas and alpacas. The wool of these animals is spun into yarn (right) and woven into warm clothes and blankets. Llamas are also used for carrying loads.

Living in the Himalayas

The Sherpas are one of the peoples living in the Himalayan kingdom of Nepal. They are used to living and working at great heights. Most people find that the thin air of the high peaks makes them sick. These Sherpas (right) are carrying loads of firewood up the mountain side. Sherpas are famous climbers and walkers and often act as guides and porters for international mountaineering expeditions and treks.

High in the Alps

The Swiss are one of the peoples living in the Alps. Swiss hill farmers raise dairy cattle. They make cheese that is famous all over the world. Each September, cheese festivals are held (below), watched by many tourists.

Farming in the mountains

Mountain sides are not the easiest places to grow crops. However many mountain peoples manage to cultivate steep slopes by cutting steps, or terraces into them.
In the Philippines (right), the terraces are flooded so that rice can be grown. The use of terraces traps soil so that it is not washed or blown away. Many mountain slopes are too steep for tractors. Sowing, harvesting and ploughing must be carried out by hand.

High-level crops

In mountainous countries, the best place to grow crops is on the lower slopes. In Japan (left) tea is a crop grown at these levels. Tea is also widely grown in India and China. In other warm lands, such as Kenya, Zimbabwe, Nicaragua or Brazil, coffee is often grown. In sunny regions of Europe, such as Italy, the lower slopes of mountains are often used as vineyards, for growing grapes.
On the higher slopes of mountains, the soil is often poor, and the growing season is very short. Potatoes and beans may be grown, and hardy grain crops such as millet, barley and buckwheat.

Grass of the Alps

These farmers in the Austrian Alps (left) are making hay. The sweet mountain grass is cut and then laid out on long racks in the fields. Here, it dries in the sun. It is then gathered up and stored in barns. It will be used as fodder for cattle during the cold months of winter. In many mountainous lands, farmers now rely on tourism to bring in extra cash.

Mountain herds

In many mountain areas, farmers raise animals instead of growing crops. Sheep and goats, which are mountain animals in the wild, are ideal for highland farming. In mountainous areas of the British Isles, such as Scotland and Wales, sheep may outnumber people by three to one. Some breeds of sheep are especially suited to the harsh weather. Cattle farming also takes place in the mountains. The Highland cattle of Scotland have long, shaggy coats to keep out the winter winds. The yaks of Tibet (right) are also well designed for the really bitter weather of the Himalayas. Less hardy cattle spend winters in valley farms.

Castles and forts

Burg Katz, Germany

Mountains are not always the easiest places to live. They are often hard to reach. However they are easy places to defend. In ancient Europe, hill forts were being built thousands of years ago. When enemies invaded, people would take refuge in these high places. Later, castles were often built on peaks, where they were hard to attack. Soldiers could control the surrounding countryside.

Away from the world

Holy people from many religions have often chosen to live far from the everyday world, in lonely places. Here, they can find the peace they need to pray and meditate. Monasteries and convents are often built high in the mountains. At the monasteries of Meteora, in Greece (left), monks had to be hauled up in baskets. Today, steps are cut into the rocks. In Tibet there are Buddhist monasteries, high in the Himalayas. About 900 years ago a hospice was founded by Christian monks high in the Alps, on the Grand St Bernard Pass. The monks and their dogs saved the lives of many travellers.

Housing for all weather

Because transport can be difficult in mountainous areas, building materials must be found locally. They may include timber from the coniferous forests, or stone quarried from the rock face. In this village in the Swiss Alps, the houses are made of timber. The windows have shutters to keep out the winter cold, and the sloping roofs are designed to cope with heavy snowfalls. They overhang the walls, so that falling snow does not pile up against doors and windows. Mountain farms often include winter shelter for animals.

Mountain cities

Kathmandu (left) is the capital city of Nepal. It is the gateway to the mighty peaks of the Himalayas. Some cities are very high indeed. Lhasa, in Tibet, is at 3684 metres above sea-level. La Paz, in Bolivia is at 3631 metres, in the Andes. A Chinese town called Wenchuan is the world's highest, at 5100 metres above sea-level.
Modern engineering methods have made it easier to build roads into areas such as Tibet. Even so, the going is often rough. The easiest way to reach mountain regions is by air.

Power from the torrent

People make use of mountains in many ways. The water which runs down mountain sides with such great force is used to make electricity. Mountain lakes and rivers may be dammed. The Colorado River (right) carries water from the Rocky Mountains. Its waters power huge screws called turbines, which drive the machinery to generate, or make, electricity. Sometimes a high mountain lake may be linked to turbines far below by a bore hole. The water from the lake may be released when power is needed. Power produced in such ways is called hydroelectric.

Mining the rocks

Mount Tom Price, in Western Australia (below), is mined for its iron ore. Mountains contain many kinds of ores, precious metals and stones for quarrying. They may be mined underground, or dug from the surface in opencast mines.

Timber!

Mountain regions are often densely forested. Firs, pines and other trees are used to supply us with timber. Some forests are natural, while others have been planted for this purpose. The trees are cut down and taken to mills. They are used to make furniture or paper. New trees must be planted to replace the old, or the mountain side will soon become eroded and lose its soil.

Eyes on the sky

Mountain summits are sometimes used as the sites for observatories. Large telescopes are set up in these buildings to study the stars. The Earth is surrounded by gases and dust. High on a mountain top, the view of the sky is much clearer than below. Mauna Kea in Hawaii (below) is at 2400 metres.

Zigzags and passes

Roads built up the sides of steep mountains have to wind from side to side in zig-zags. Drivers must take special care on these 'hairpin' bends (right). They may need to put snow chains on their tyres to help them grip the road. Mountain passes may be closed in winter. Roads are often at risk from falling rocks, land slides and falls of snow known as avalanches. Roofs may be built across sections of road to provide shelter. The highest road is in China. It crosses one pass at 5632 metres.

Bridges and tunnels

Mountain roads and railways need to cross valleys and pass through mountains. High bridges, or viaducts (below), carry them over deep gorges. Tunnels are bored through long sections of solid rock. The world's longest road tunnel is the St Gotthard, in the Swiss Alps. It is over 16 kilometres long, and took 11 years to build.

Mountain transport

In the Andes, there are some of the highest railway lines in the world (right). One in Peru was built 4817 metres above sea level. Many have special tracks. A cog, or pinion, under the train fits into a slotted rail, or rack.

Along the line

Cable cars can be used to carry small groups of people to the summit of a mountain. The tourists (below left) are travelling to the top of Sugar Loaf Mountain from the city of Rio de Janeiro, in Brazil.

Winter sports

Many tourists visit the mountains to enjoy the scenery or to ski (right). Chair lifts carry skiers up to the best slopes. Skiing has become a major sport. People compete cross-country, downhill, or over a winding course in the 'slalom' events. Ski jumping is the most spectacular of all mountain sports, followed closely by bobsledding.

Challenge of the rockface

Rock climbing is another sport that has become very popular. Beginners learn how to find hand and footholds in a rock face. They learn how to use ropes and to work as a team. Above all, they learn to climb safely without risking life and limb. Climbing is dangerous, but it is very exciting. To many people, the challenge of the rock face is the ultimate test. Some climbers tackle the world's highest and most difficult peaks. They may need to take oxygen on the high slopes in order to breath properly in the thin air.

Expeditions need careful planning. Equipment must be carried up to the starting point, or base camp. New camps are set up as the expedition advances up the mountain. At the last one, climbers prepare for the final assault on the summit. They may have to sleep rough, or bivouac, on the way.

The great outdoors

You don't have to hang from a rope over a precipice in order to enjoy the mountains! Many people like to hike over mountain trails (right). Other outdoor pursuits include mountain running, mountain cycling, and white-water rafting and canoeing. Many mountainous areas are run as national parks or as wildlife reserves. They offer unspoilt nature in the wild.

Mountain rescue

If you do go walking in the mountains, make sure that you are properly equipped and well prepared. The weather can change very quickly. Mists can come down, or storms can break. You may get lost. The first rule is always to tell people where you are going and when you hope to return. The second is to wear the right clothes. Be prepared for wet and cold even if it is sunny when you set out. Wear proper boots. Carry food and hot drinks. Also take a map, a torch, and a compass. Rescue teams are trained to search with dogs for lost or injured climbers. They may use planes (left) or helicopters.

The record breakers

★ The highest mountain in North America is Mt Mckinley, in Alaska's Denali National Park. It is 6194 metres above sea level.

★ The tallest peak in Western Europe is Mont Blanc, which lies between France and Italy. It is 4810 metres high. The tallest in Eastern Europe is Mt Elbruz, in the Soviet republic of Georgia, at 5633 metres. The highest, mountain in the British Isles is Ben Nevis, in Scotland, at 1347 metres.

★ The highest point in Australia is Mt Kosciusko (2228 metres). New Zealand's highest is Mt Cook (3764 metres).

★ The highest mountain in Asia is also the world's highest. Mt Everest or Qomolangma is 8863 metres high. It rises on the border between Tibet and Nepal. The peak known as K2 was also a contender for the record.

Mount Everest

- Mount Everest was first climbed on 29 May 1953, by the New Zealander Edmund Hillary and the Sherpa Tenzing Norgay. The first woman to climb Everest was Junko Tabei of Japan, in 1975. The most frequent climber has been the Sherpa Sundare, with five ascents to his credit.

- The world's highest plateau is Tibet, in China. Over an area of 200 000 square kilometres, the average height is 4875 metres above sea level.

- The world's highest range is formed by the Himalaya and the Karakoram. It contains nine peaks over 8000 metres.

Sherpa Tenzing Norgay at the summit of Mount Everest in June 1953.

Mount Cook, New Zealand

Index

The numbers in **bold** are illustrations.

Africa 8, 9, 12, 13
Alaska 28
alpacas 16
America 4, 6, 9, 11, 12, 14, 28
Asia 12, 13, 28
Australia 15, 22, 28
Austria 15, 19
avalanches 24

Bakhtiari 16, **16**
bears 11
  grizzlies 11, **11**
birds 12, 13
  Alpine chough 13, **13**
  Andean condor 12, **12**
  golden eagles 12, **12**
  ptarmigan 12
  wallcreeper 13, **13**
block mountains 3, **3**
Bolivia 21
Brazil 18, 25

cable cars 25, **25**
Canada 7, 11, 14
castles 20, **20**
cattle 8
cheese festivals 17, **17**
China 10, 13, 15, 21, 24, 29
climate 8, 9
climbing 17, 26
crops 8, **8**

dams 22, **22**
deserts 9

Earth 2, 3, 4
Equator 8
erosion 7, 18, 23
expeditions 17, 26

farming 18-19, **18,** 21
faults 3, **3**
fjords 7, **7**
forests 8, 23
  coniferous 8, **8,** 11, 21

rain 8, **8**
fossils 3
France 15

geology 3, 4
glaciers 6, **6**
goats 10, 11
  ibex 10, **10**
gorges 24

herding 16
Hillary, Edmund 29
houses 21, **21**
hydroelectric power 22

Ice Ages 6, 7
Incas 14
Iran 16
Italy 15, 18

Japan 15, 18, **18,** 29

Kenya 8, 18
Kathmandu 21, **21**

lakes 7, 22
land slides 24
La Paz 21
lava 4, 5
Lhasa 21
llamas 16

Machu Picchu 14, **14**
magma 2, 4
mining 22, **22**
monasteries 20
  Meteora 20, **20**
mountain grass 19, **19**
mountain peaks
  Ben Nevis 28
  K2 28
  Kilimanjaro 8, **8**
  Mont Blanc 28
  Mount Cook 28, **29**
  Mount Elbruz 28

30

Mount Everest 7, 13, 28, **28**
Mount Kenya 9
Mount Kosciusko 28
Mount Mckinley 28
Mount St Helens 4, **4**
Mount Tom Price 22, **22**
Sugar Loaf Mountain 25
mountain ranges 2
  Alps 15, **15,** 17, 19, 20, 21, **21,** 24
  Altai 11
  Andes 14, 16, 21, 25
  Appalachians 14
  Atlas 13
  Cascade 9
  Caucasus 15
  Great Dividing 15
  Himalayas 10, 11, 13, 14, **14,** 15, 17, 20, 21, 28, 29
  Hindu Kush 11
  Karakoram 15, 29
  Parnir 15
  Pyrenees 15
  Rockies 11, 22
  Sierra Madre 14
  Sierra Nevada 9
  Urals 15
  Zagros 16
mountain rescue 27, **27**
mountain safety 27
mud slides 4

Nepal 17, 21, 29
New Zealand 7, 15, 28, 29
Nicaragua 18
Norway 7, **7**

observatories 23
  Mauna Kea 23, **23**

Pacific Ocean 9
Pakistan 7
passes 24
  Grand St Bernard 20
Peru 25
Philippines 18, **18**

plants 9, 11
plateaux 29
  Tibetan 10

Quechua 16, **16**

rabbits 12
railways 24, 25, **25**
rain 9
Rio de Janeiro 25
rivers 22
  Colorado 22, **22**
  Mercedc 6
roads 21, 24
  hairpin bends 24, **24**

satellites 2
sheep 10, 11, 16
Sherpas 17, **17**
  Sundare 29
  Tenzing Norgay 29, **29**
Spain 13, 15
sports 26-7
Sun 7
Switzerland 17

Tabei, Junko 29
Tanzania 8
Tibet 20, 21, 28, 29
tourism 19
tunnels 24, **24**
  St Gotthard 24

USSR 15, 28

viaducts 24, **24**
volcanoes 2, 4-5, **4, 5**
  extinct 5
  Fujiyama 15, **15**

Wenchuan 21

yaks 10, **10**
Yosemite 6, **6**

31

HEINEMANN CHILDREN'S REFERENCE
a division of Heinemann Educational Books Ltd
Halley Court, Jordan Hill, Oxford OX2 8EJ

OXFORD LONDON EDINBURGH
MELBOURNE SYDNEY AUCKLAND
MADRID ATHENS BOLOGNA
SINGAPORE IBADAN NAIROBI HARARE
GABORONE KINGSTON PORTSMOUTH NH(USA)

ISBN 0 431 00930 9

A CIP catalogue record for this book
is available from the British Library

© Heinemann Educational Books Ltd 1990
First published 1990

All rights reserved: no part of this publication
may be reproduced, stored in a retrieval system,
or transmitted in any form or by any means, electronic,
mechanical, photocopying, recording, or otherwise,
without the prior written permission of the Publishers.

Design by Julian Holland Publishing Ltd
Cover concept by Groom and Pickerill

Printed in Hong Kong

90 91 92 93 94 95 10 9 8 7 6 5 4 3 2 1

Acknowledgements
Illustrations: BLA Publishing Limited.
Photographs: $a = above$ $m = middle$ $b = below$
2a ZEFA; 3b J.G. James/Seaphot; 4a, 4b ZEFA; 5b John Lythgoe/Seaphot; 6a Douglas Dickens; 6b The Hutchison Library; 7a Douglas Dickens; 7b The Hutchison Library; 8a ZEFA; 9b R.J. Hart; 10a Claudio Galasso/Seaphot; 10b The Hutchison Library; 11a Ardea; 11b John Waters/Seaphot; 12a J.Jeffery/NHPA; 12b South American Pictures; 13a, 13b Brian Hawkes/NHPA; 14a Ivor Edmonds/Seaphot; 14b South American Pictures; 15a, 15b ZEFA; 16a Susan Griggs Agency; 16b Douglas Dickens; 17a ZEFA; 17b Swiss National Tourist Office; 18a ZEFA; 18b Douglas Dickens; 19a N.A. Callow/NHPA; 19b The Hutchison Library; 20a Topham Picture Library; 20b Douglas Dickens; 21a ZEFA; 21b Ed Rotberg; 22a, 22b, 23a ZEFA; 23b Science Photo Library; 24a ZEFA; 24b Swiss National Tourist Office; 25a South American Pictures; 25b, 26a, 26b ZEFA; 27a Canadian High Commission; 27b, 28 ZEFA; 29a Topham Picture Library; 29b Robert Harding.